$1 50

Your England Revisited

Contents

Acknowledgements

Photograph 1 comes from the United States Information Service, photograph 13A from Reece Winstone, photograph 43 from the Council for the Preservation of Rural England, photograph 55 from J. Allan Cash.

The remainder were taken from the files of the *Architectural Review* and *Architects' Journal*. Nearly all of the ground shots I took myself. The aerial views are due to the skill of William J. Toomey, who kept the camera steady despite indifferent weather and the uneven flying of

IAN NAIRN

The publishers wish to acknowledge their indebtedness to Mr Denys Thompson, whose pamphlet Your England *was the inspiration of the present book.*

Your England Revisited

THIS book is trying to say something very simple—that every bit of the visible world can be exciting, expressive and individual. That a street corner, a bit of grass, a town square, can make you gasp with joy. That your particular street corner, or the view from your window, or the roundabout down the road, ought to make you gasp with joy.

Does it? If you are very lucky, and live in Regent's Park or Oxford or parts of the North Riding, then it might. But the morning journey is mostly past a bumbling chaotic dribble of objects, dumped down without thought and without love. Be cruel to dogs and children and you end up in court. Be cruel to the environment, and the relevant committee will most probably commend a 'valuable amenity'. Every time that somebody hurts a landscape or a townscape he is being loveless and stupid and arrogant.

Many of the wounds are made by public bodies—in the name of the public, in *your* name—without even the human excuse of wanting to make a profit. Many, also, are done blindly, so that the crime is thoughtlessness—but the hurt remains the same. If somebody out of mistaken kindness lays out the churchyard as a flower garden, and reduces something noble and grand to something fussy and mean, then it doesn't matter in the least how well intentioned they were. Good intentions are not enough.

What is enough? Simply the ability to see every town and village—and every significant part of them—as individual places, just as though they were people. And just like people—or your friends, at any rate—to give them all the individual treatment they demand.

Different places, different treatments: circumstances alter cases. This is the foundation of English common-law freedom and tolerance; but anathema to almost all town-planning officials, multiple-store owners, public servants, local officers. A false equality has replaced it, insisting that every place must be treated alike up to that arbitrary line, the borough boundary. Next door is another borough, with its own arbitrary rules: two ostriches with heads deep in the sand. Boundary junctions like this can be funny, sometimes. But it is a sick joke.

And a sick situation produces it. Make no mistake, this is a fight for our lives as human beings. Not in a shallow political sense, as though a swing left or a swing right is going to change anything, but at the deepest level of our own being.

If you let your town become characterless then you erode your own character by the same amount. If you are born in a characterless place, then a crime has been done to you, a little like being born malformed. Most people recover, but some do not—and why should it have happened at all?

The only way out is to think and feel for yourselves. Look at each site individually, feel its own character. Not necessarily 'beauty', because the character may be grim or wild or austere. Hence the argument that 'beauty is in the eye of the beholder', which is used so often as an alibi for failing to think or feel, does not apply. This business is like Alexander Pope's 'something previous e'en to taste—'tis sense'. The taste can come afterwards: it is the basic 'sense' of places that is at stake. By analogy, there can be any number of opinions on whether my own hands and feet are beautiful. Most of the opinions are unfavourable, but they all agree that the objects *are* hands and feet, and that there is a difference between the two. This is the basic 'sense' of the objects; and towns are as different from each other as hands, feet, ears or noses. Useless to apply to an ear an ointment which is intended for sore feet; and useless—criminally stupid—to apply to one town what may have been perfectly well suited to the next.

This business of diagnosing a town's needs, rather on the lines of a medical diagnosis, is not difficult. More than anything else it needs an open, responsive, tolerant-feeling heart, prepared to do for another place what it would not enjoy doing for itself. The intellect is in many ways a drawback, but an open heart is an enormous advantage. Use it, before outside pressures stop it up. Feel with it, make the brain work for the heart (instead of the other way round), look at every single part of every single street, understand the difference between places.

If we don't do this, and do it quickly, then a whole segment of life will slip back into brutish existence. If you live on the outskirts of any large town it is a fair bet that your environment is already a witless chaos—a dumping down of every kind of man-made object, urban, suburban and sub-rural, with no relationship to each other or to the site. A new ugly word was needed to describe it, so I coined one: 'subtopia'. It has already produced a pattern of behaviour over which earnest town-planners and sociologists wring their hands. 'We provided the best,' they say, 'and it is misused.' They are mistaken. They provided the physical needs—hygienic drains and enough daylight—and ignored the spiritual needs. Where the nineteenth-century slums crippled bodies, these more insidious twentieth-century slums are crippling minds—your minds.

And if it is bad in Britain it is twenty times worse in America. There the whole man-made world has exploded; cities can literally be a hundred miles across, every urban and rural pattern has been submerged in an endless watery gruel.

No need to build fall-out shelters in this first illustration—an air view of Los Angeles—for in effect the H-bomb has happened already. Woe betide those who did it, and heaven help those who live in it. Including us.

1

Los Angeles, U.S.A., outskirts

And yet it needn't be like this, in spite of the motor-car, in spite of modern space standards. Here is identity at its simplest:

2

Whitby, Yorks, N.R.

Whitby, in Yorkshire, a unique arrangement of buildings, site and function. It could be no other place. Yet although this example happens to be centuries old, the will to make places is new-born in everyone. The need for some sort of relationship is a basic part of life. It need not be an artificial chumminess; it can be austere or intimate or impassive, according to the needs of the place: but *some* act of relationship there must be. This is the chief town-planning problem: to bring every part of the landscape or townscape into accord. And not a forced accord, or something that the designer wants to impose from outside, but the solution that comes naturally from the particular circumstances and may work nowhere else.

3

Hull

But the modern 'solution' is usually this—an endless spatter of separate units, with nothing brought together or related: an environment macedoine. All the physical refinements may be there, but what is there for the heart and mind to feed on?

The ground view corresponding to 4 is inescapable. Every town in Britain has edges looking something like this:

6

Carlisle (1954)

. . . which spread a little more every year. That was the edge of Carlisle in 1954.

By 1960 the new edge looked like this . . .

7

Carlisle (1960)

. . . another piece of chaos made visible, half a mile further down the road. There is nothing wrong with people wanting houses and gardens. What is wrong is the way they are arranged; or, rather, not arranged. Lack of relationship all the time.

So the problem becomes one of tying the knots of relationship: of combining, uniting, bringing together, of selecting the important things and enhancing the differences between places. And, as a genius once said: 'not any old differences, but the significant ones'. If Jones has big ears and Smith has small ones, that is undoubtedly a difference; but unless it has affected their essential identities, the difference is not significant. And the problem is not only a large-scale one affecting whole towns, but something which is part of every square inch of the earth's surface. A single building can show lack of identity:

8

Faced with a characterful building on either side, it is as if this one took fright, was brainwashed—and then forgot to inscribe anything else on the cleaned slate. This is nothingness made manifest.

Every street corner can show a similarly careless and loveless collection of objects thrown down aimlessly. No co-ordination between the parts means no identity in the whole. Where are you? Anywhere. Nowhere.

9

Anywhere—Nowhere

10

Stretham, Isle of Ely

Yet just such ordinary units can be combined into something as intricate and exciting as the art of fugue (or a good bit of jazz, because there are no 'brows' in this game). Here two cottages set up the main theme, one at ninety degrees is in counterpoint, and the garden shed forms a half-size echo. This is all accidental and instinctive, but no less of an achievement; our job now is to do this deliberately and consciously with every single part of the environment.

In the end the problem can be put even more simply, as a matter of making a pattern out of one window surround, or even out of three objects in a shop window, two glass bowls and a ship's log. At this level the point seems natural and obvious, but it is exactly the same pattern that underlies the design of a city square or of a whole city or region.

11

Lowestoft

12

Loughborough Road, South London

Pattern and arrangement need not mean regimented order. These L.C.C. blocks of flats, admirable though they may be individually, are assembled in a naive, box-of-bricks, geometrical way, imposing a formality and simplicity on life which it does not possess. The true pattern, which will be different for each place, is much more organic and complex. Formality is fine for formal occasions, but not otherwise—a good servant but a bad master.

In particular, there are town ways and country ways of doing everything, and only a blind man would put down an object without taking account of its environment. Advertising in the country, except of the most personal sort ('Fresh farm eggs 5s. 6d. per dozen'), is a pointless intrusion of urban man; though even here the virtually impossible can be achieved by personal attention to the surroundings, as the French Dubonnet and St. Raphael advertisements can show. But advertising in a town is a completely natural expression of urban life, and many places could do with not less but more of it, as long as it is fitted to the surroundings. In these two views of the same street in Bristol, 13, taken in 1910 and 1957, it is the older view which has greater identity and pattern by a long way—yet it carries more advertising, not less.

13

Bristol, 1910 above and 1957 below

Everything hangs on the way the advertising is done. A few of the New Town centres have begun to grasp the idea, though in a wretchedly timid way.

14

Harlow New Town

And at the hub of the metropolis, hubbub of noise and bustle, the advertising can be a hubbub too:

15

Piccadilly Circus

This would be ridiculously overbearing in Harlow, just as 14 would be far too demure for Piccadilly. Each place sets its own standards and must be treated on its own terms. But neither is an excuse for the mass-produced advertisement jammed down on the scene without a look at the surroundings, or for the too tardy twinge of conscience that makes confusion worse confounded by putting a tiny out-of-place flower garden in front of it. Neither ad. nor garden is wrong in itself; both are very wrong in the particular situation.

16

Northwich

17

Banstead

The effect of applying one stereotyped treatment to every street in a borough is ludicrously shown here by the footpath and the gawky lamp-standards striding inappropriately across Banstead Common.

A country footpath can be treated in rural terms (this example on the very edge of Harlow New Town is as admirable as it is unexpected) . . .

18

. . . or it can be stamped out according to the book of bye-laws without a thought for the surroundings, as has been done in this case in the middle of Cumberland.

19

Again, a country bus-stop should not be an ungainly pole set down without thought.

London Transport sign in Kent

20A

20B

Bus-stop in Derbyshire

It can be managed with much less fuss, though just as effectively, if a little care is used. It becomes an inflection to the view instead of an imposition on it.

This is such a little thing, such an easy habit to get into, yet in the end it is one of the most important things life has got to teach. If neglected, the result is a barbarous horror like this:

Witney, Oxon

21A

Stratton Audley, Oxon

applied to natural objects which ought to look like this. And this in England, the home of nature-lovers!

21B

Each of these designs is expressive of its own surroundings; a rough wooden seat for the North Riding valley:

22

Low Fell, Yorks, N.R.

. . . an exquisite and elegant shape for the sophisticated Zürich pleasure park:

23

Zürich

Imagine the absurdity that would result if they were to be transposed—the chic seat in the North Riding, the rough one in the Swiss park.

And equally, with this pair of roads, all the details go to tell you the type of place. In one case, trim spick-and-span suburbia . . .

24

Camilla Lacey, near Dorking

. . . in the other case, the rough rural countryside. Each scene speaks through all its parts, just as a really complete personality will express itself in every part of its being—dress, speech and feeling.

25

Road between Norwich and Loddon

26

Oxford skyline

In every view there are important and essential things whose impact must not be blurred. It is absurd to stamp the superb skyline of Oxford with a forest of street lights and signs so that you see concrete posts first and towers and spires second. Street lighting is not bad in itself (though there is not much to be said for the design of this lamp-post); it becomes bad if it dominates where it should be subordinate. The engineers here were simply applying a standard 25 ft. column height quite blindly: roadside strip illumination would have done just as well. There should be much more flexibility, with the understanding that no part of the landscape exists in a vacuum: everything is interdependent. And if the bye-laws do not allow of this flexibility, then the bye-laws are wrong.

Another way of solving the problem. Most towns would have had a pole sticking out in the street and competing with the rhythm of the buildings. Here the light is mounted on the wall (just as the country bus-stop sign was attached to its surroundings and not imposed on them). And the fact that I personally think this to be a clumsy and ugly design—a matter of taste—is far less important than the basic act of relationship with the surroundings.

27

Haddington, East Lothian

Exactly the same thing is true of wires and poles. They are not bad in themselves; it is just that they may be bad in particular surroundings. When they overshadow and dwarf this Oxfordshire village street, this is a means which defeats its own ends.

28

When they are in a self-contained environment—as in this back-alley in Lowestoft—they begin to spit out a strange beauty and pattern of their own. (Any problem involving poles or posts is always going to be difficult, because of the way verticals will automatically stand out in the view.)

29

Identity has been used so far to describe the main divisions which everyone recognizes—town, country, suburb, wilderness. But in a crowded industrial country such as Britain there are many more categories.

One example is the main trunk road, which is on a scale quite different from the surrounding patterns and needs large-scale trim to go with it, as here:

30

A303, near Wylye, Wilts

. . . not the sad confusion of big and small which it so often gets.

31

A303, Sparkford, Somerset

Chandler's Ford, near Southampton

Another is the pylon landscape. Here, accidentally, this is beginning to make up a pattern in its own right, with the bold frame and the pairs of lines moving away. Unhappily it has done so in the middle of an existing rural pattern without any kind of thought or feeling. But once it is there, the only thing to do is to try to make some kind of identity for it on its own terms.

The corollary of this, of course, is that the truly non-industrial places should stay non-industrial. This view on the Isle of Wight is one of the few bits of rural coastline between Folkestone and Weymouth. An atomic power station was proposed for it: in this case the landscape loss would have far outweighed any material gain.

33

Hamstead, I.O.W.

Britain has, already, hundreds of square miles of semi-industrial or semi-urban landscape—a few trees, a few houses, a few factories, no identity. These are the areas which could be made into a positive industrial pattern, one which has immense landscape potentialities . . .

34

. . . like this view of Northfleet in Kent. The landscape of chalk-pits, pylons, old houses left almost islanded on tops of cliffs, could be tremendously exciting. Yet nobody is trying to make it so, everything is still put down piecemeal.

35

Another example of an identity which makes up its own pattern—the robust seaside resort. This is part of Blackpool, and in its own terms it is splendid (just as in other terms Mevagissey, Bournemouth and the uninhabited north-west coast of Scotland are splendid). But to make everywhere a Blackpool would be terrifying and annihilating.

The effects possible at the joins of different identities, if they are kept sharp, are superb. This view of Chichester shows cathedral and country brought right up to one another, without any draggle-tailed twilight zone. The sense of each is heightened by the effect of looking across into an obviously different environment—'here' and 'there', without any alien element from one straggling over into the other. This will not be so in Chichester much longer, alas, because a ring road is due to go through the Westgate Fields in the foreground, and though it will doubtless be carefully designed and landscaped, the basic point of the view, which is the contrast of essences, will have gone.

Here is the same point in a less familiar, less pretty, way: the view down the main street of Coleshill in Warwickshire, to the vast cooling towers of Hams Hall Power Station. In an industrialized part of Britain this is a viable pair of identities, and each gains through being contrasted with the other. But the whole proposition is blurred because the middle distance is filled with houses; instead of separate recognizable places there is one vast sub-rural and sub-urban continuum spreading over everything.

37

The most frequent kind of blurring and confusing of elements happens when, often with a guilty conscience, people feel the need to decorate or embroider the landscape or townscape. It is always fatally easy to transplant a flower garden from a suburban house, where it is admirable, into the middle of the countryside . . .

38

A34 between Oxford and Woodstock

. . . or into the centre of the town, where it looks ridiculously out of place.

Bristol

Urban parks, in fact, are all the better for being large-scale, calm and unfussy, because then they act as a foil, as an oasis in the city.

40

St. James's Park, London

Identity is always made up of relationships: of putting all the different elements in any view together to make more than just the sum of the separate objects. At its simplest, this means taking the trouble to fit a litter bin to its surroundings . . .

41

Seaton, Devon

. . . instead of allowing it to stand around disconnectedly in the view. (In this example, in the middle of Cumberland, the bin is far worse than the litter it was intended to prevent, and to hoist a pompous sign high above it is quite preposterous.)

42

A6 between Penrith and Carlisle

And, of course, every single person can contribute his own act of relationship by not subscribing to a view like this. Even here, the courteous well-intentioned notice is another piece of litter.

43

Official departments, particularly the Services, are often apt to leave much more tangible and permanent pieces of litter around the countryside. This is just man fouling his own nest: here, he is not only no better than the animals, he is nowhere near their level.

44

Calveley, Cheshire

Every man-made alteration to the environment has the choice of being built haphazardly or with consideration. A roadside filling station can be a collection of unrelated signs and pumps . . .

North Wales

. . . or the elements can be made into a pattern with meaning (not just 'tidied up'):

46

Isle of Man

Ironically, the second example is probably more effective as an advertising eye-catcher than the first.

47

Rugeley

Similarly with roundabouts. There is no point in stuffing them full of redundant and sometimes contradictory signs, when the business of clear road directions should have been completed long before.

48

Como

This Italian example—not intended to be a direct comparison—is simple, elegant and cheap, and can be moved about easily to suit different kinds of traffic flow. British traffic officials often seem to have forgotten the meaning of this kind of flexibility altogether. Perhaps that is one reason why life on the Continent is so much more fun.

Bury St. Edmunds

How many times do we have to say the same thing? The original Victorian lamp, set against its white painted niche, is a genuine bit of imaginative design, making a virtue out of necessity, which seems to be quite beyond us today.

A2 near Sittingbourne, Kent

Our intellectual habits are so strong that we sometimes try to make the whole landscape into a legal document. The final consequence of this would be to paint 'field' on a field to make sure that it has legal standing. The blindness of this attitude shows a terrifying isolation and splitting-up of life which goes much deeper than simply putting up stupid signs.

The mania for putting everything into words seems to be a British disease. This street sign in Amsterdam, for example, conveys a complex set of facts—expressed in an international code—yet conveys them in *visual*, not literary, terms. A piece of music is not a book, a street view is not a legal paragraph.

51

Relationship between old and new in the landscape is almost as important as between old and young in a family. Old buildings can be killed with neglect, and they can be killed with the wrong sort of kindness, by surrounding them with mock half-timbering, for example, or setting them aside in a sterilized 'cultural zone'. What they need is respect without subservience, neatly shown in these recent flats on Chelsea Embankment, which take up the patterns of the Georgian terrace but express them in a purely twentieth-century way.

52

So flats can be sordid . . .

61

Woodberry Down, London

. . . or elegant:

62

Ham Common, Surrey

. . . and houses can create a repetitive unending desert . . .

63

Luton

... or a delightful miniature village:

64

Roehampton

65

Biggin Hill

. . . and shacks and transport caffs can make a worthwhile pattern too. Anything can be made expressive, part of a coherent and exciting environment. Always, not *what* but *how*.

66

Northfleet

The largest part of 'How' in the housing problem is making the different parts of the environment interlock, letting no odd corners be wasted. This does not mean cramming things in, but simply ensuring that every bit of the landscape is used positively. Greater co-operation is needed between all the multifarious public bodies which affect the land surface—councils, boards, authorities, departments.

67

This view of part of Edinburgh has fragments of about a dozen different uses, all carried out in isolation—housing, ring road, hospital, quarry, playing fields. These same uses could have been related and interlocked.

And there are hundreds of places like this all over Britain which could take four or five times as many people simply by filling in all the gaps:

68

Cross Hands, near Swansea

Here is part of a new estate near Bristol—indifferent design, wasted space, no thought and no love; a wilderness. No wonder there are Teddy Boys.

69

Multiple use of land can go right down to the smallest things, like this railing in Zürich which is a cycle rack as well . . .

70

. . . or the street in Westminster where the awnings of the shops protect the stalls too:

71

This is living together, with everybody part of the environment—not one stereo-typed or over-tidy sort of environment, but what the specific needs and specific conditions demand.

Sometimes formality—but not everywhere:

72

Hove

Sometimes informality, where this seems appropriate:

73

Sidmouth

And modern clean industry not shunted off into a separate zone . . .

74

Harlow New Town

... when it should be an acknowledged part of life, and can be worked into a street as easily and comfortably as this:

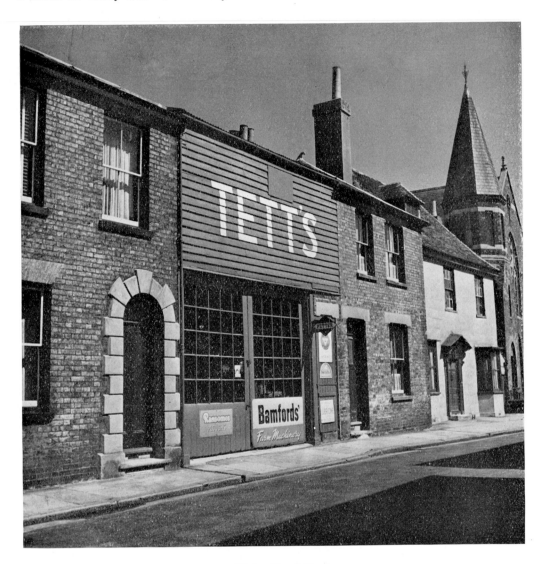

75

Holt, Norfolk

76

Kingston-on-Thames

A whole place, different from any other place. Market, town hall, church and shops all brought together, not isolated. This is what we have got to achieve . . .

. . . for the alternative in the end is this . . .

77

Chicago, U.S.A.

. . . which is a kind of death. There is no one rule or set of rules. The only guide is the individual circumstances of individual places and people, and the wish always to create identity and relationship: a humane, exciting, integrated environment.

Posers

The next section is a bit of do-it-yourself. In each case, I have tried to get to the essence of the view or the place. If there were conflicting essences, I have tried to decide which was important. My views—which may not be yours at all—are suggested very briefly on pages 123–4. Don't worry about them, just feel yourself into the needs of the place and make up your own mind whether the poser is harmonious or discordant, able to be itself or submerged under an alien personality.

2

4

9

8

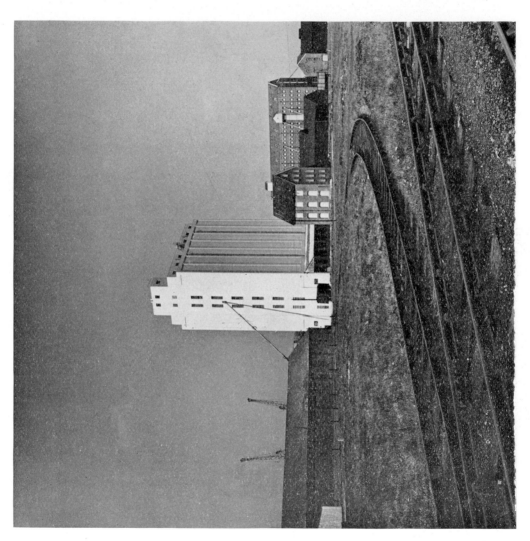

12

[100]

14

16

After

Before

20

[108]

22

26

28

32

Clues to Posers

1   Ruined but still alive; Pickworth, near Stamford

2   The bend means everything; Tissington, Derbyshire

3   Rough stuff; Sheepstor, Dartmoor

4   More than some cathedrals; temple of Xanadu at Oakengates, Shropshire

5   Wreck a town, and give it a fancy name; Nottingham

6   Straight talking and no fuss; Alkmaar, Holland

7   Countryside meets town; Wareham, Dorset

8   Make your own landscape—worth a town-planning medal; gypsy caravan near Bentley, Hants

9   Cover the land with statistical units; Basingstoke, Surrey

10   Industry on its own terms; Sharpness, Glos

11   Big factory that fits into the village, small houses that don't; Wolvercote, near Oxford

12   Steaming grandeur, the mills of God; Corby, Northants

13   Decent river, decent building, misguided gardening; Salford, Lancs

14   No words needed; Autoroute near Ghent, Belgium

15   Advertising adds interest? Holt, Norfolk

16   This should be the centre of town not a flower-garden; Stone, Staffs

17   Not gasholders, but a miracle; back of St. Pancras station, London

18   End of the world; Kingston By-Pass, Surrey

19   No excuses needed for this pylon; Aust, Glos

20   Before: a real pub. After: done up to be fashionable; Littlehampton, Sussex

21   Get the priorities straight; entrance to Royal Military Academy, Sandhurst

22   The new lighting will be bigger, newer, and better; Treforest estate, near Pontypridd, Glam

23   Each part alive and expressive; Isle of Man

24   A private dream made public: it won't work; Purley, Surrey

25   Green Belt? Mitcham Common, Surrey

26   Rough ways may well be best; near Loddon, Norfolk

27   Roads and fields in harmony; near Falkirk, Scotland

28   What about the shapes and contour? Thirlmere, Lake District

29   Pipelines rammed on to the landscape; Loch Sloy, Scotland

30   The wild places; above Killin, Scotland

31   Chalk and cheese fitting together; Kirkcaldy, Fife

32   A place for everything, and this is the place; Blackpool, Lancs

33   A traditional scene, but everything new; Harlow New Town, Essex